SPORTS ALL-STARS

LEBRON JAMES

Jon M. Fishman

Lerner Publications ◆ Minneapolis

Lerner Publications Company
A division of Lerner Publishing Group, Inc.
241 First Avenue North
Minneapolis, MN 55401 USA

For reading levels and more information, look up this title at www.lernerbooks.com.

Main body text set in Albany Std 15/22. Typeface provided by Agfa.

Library of Congress Cataloging-in-Publication Data

Names: Fishman, Jon M., author.
Title: Lebron James / Jon M. Fishman.
Description: Minneapolis : Lerner Publications, [2017] | Series: Sports all-stars |
    Includes bibliographical references and index.
Identifiers: LCCN 2016048117 (print) | LCCN 2017003423 (ebook) | ISBN
    9781512434521 (lb : alk. paper) | ISBN 9781512456172 (pb : alk. paper) | ISBN
    9781512450866 (eb pdf)
Subjects: LCSH: James, LeBron—Juvenile literature. | Basketball players—United
    States—Biography—Juvenile literature. | African American basketball players—
    Biography—Juvenile literature.
Classification: LCC GV884.J36 F57 2017 (print) | LCC GV884.J36 (ebook) | DDC
    796.323092 [B] —dc23

LC record available at https://lccn.loc.gov/2016048117

Manufactured in the United States of America
1-42101-25395-3/16/2017

CONTENTS

The Golden State Warriors couldn't stop LeBron James during the 2016 championship game.

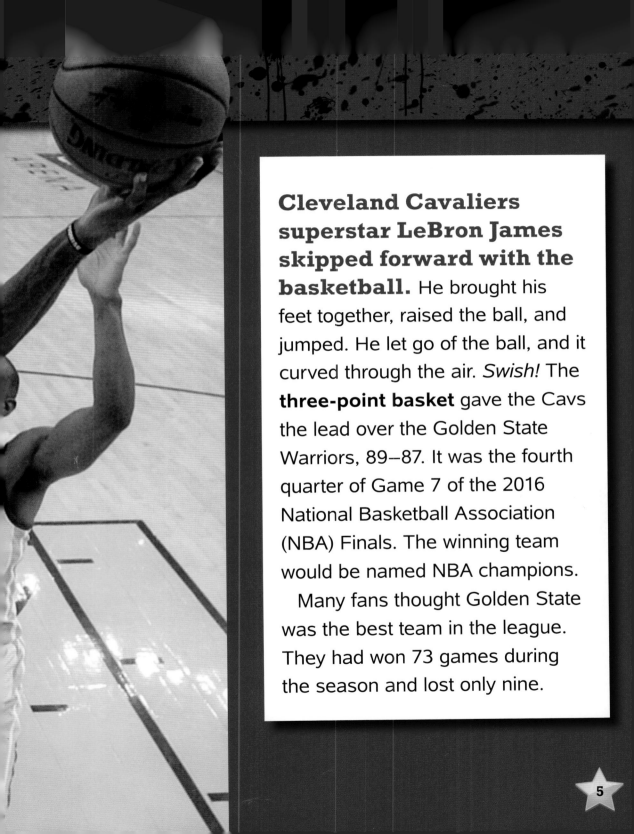

Cleveland Cavaliers superstar LeBron James skipped forward with the basketball. He brought his feet together, raised the ball, and jumped. He let go of the ball, and it curved through the air. *Swish!* The **three-point basket** gave the Cavs the lead over the Golden State Warriors, 89–87. It was the fourth quarter of Game 7 of the 2016 National Basketball Association (NBA) Finals. The winning team would be named NBA champions.

Many fans thought Golden State was the best team in the league. They had won 73 games during the season and lost only nine.

That was the best record in NBA history. They took an early lead in the Finals, winning three games to one. But Cleveland won Games 5 and 6 to tie the series. It all came down to Game 7. The arena in Oakland, California, was packed with cheering people. More than 30 million more fans watched on TV.

There were 4 minutes, 52 seconds left on the game clock when James sank his three-point basket. Golden State tied the game a few seconds later. Then neither team scored for almost four minutes. With 53 seconds left in the quarter, Kyrie Irving hit a three-pointer to give the Cavs the lead. Then James made a **free throw** to make the score 93–89. Time ran out. Cleveland won the NBA championship!

James is an NBA champion, and he's also an Olympic champion. He first played for Team USA at the 2004 Olympics in Athens, Greece. The team finished third, but James and his teammates won gold in 2008 and 2012. James chose not to play in 2016.

James (center) holds up the championship trophy after beating the Golden State Warriors in the 2016 NBA Finals.

This was the third time James had won the NBA Finals. But it was the first time he had done it as a member of the Cavs. Winning the title with Cleveland was special. James had grown up in nearby Akron, Ohio.

Fans, coaches, and reporters streamed onto the court after the game. James hugged his teammates. Then he fell to his hands and knees and cried with joy. "Cleveland, this is for you," he said.

"THE CHOSEN ONE"

James signs copies of his book at a bookstore in Ohio.

"I first started playing basketball when I was about 9 [years old]," James wrote in a book about his childhood. Before that he played football. He liked football because he could score touchdowns. He was still too short to **dunk** a basketball.

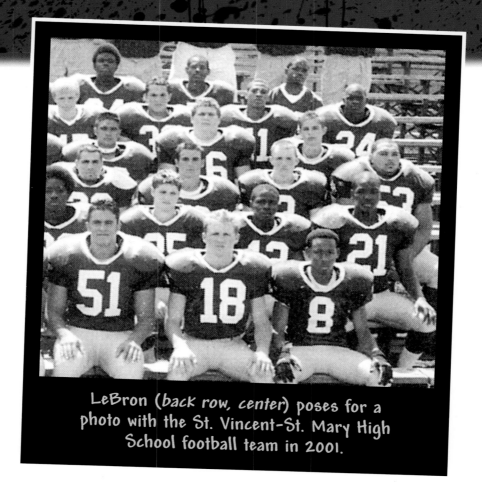

LeBron (back row, center) poses for a photo with the St. Vincent-St. Mary High School football team in 2001.

It didn't take LeBron long to grow into basketball. He was tall and strong by the time he reached St. Vincent-St. Mary (SVSM) High School in Akron. From there, his basketball career took off like a rocket. As a freshman in 1999–2000, he averaged 21 points per game. The team lost just once all year and won the state title.

The team won the state championship again in 2000–2001. LeBron was even better than he had been the year before. Fans and **scouts** around the country were taking notice. He appeared on the February 18, 2002, cover of *Sports Illustrated*. The headline read, "The Chosen One."

The honors and big games kept coming. He scored 50 points in one game. Then he scored 52 points in a game SVSM won, 78–52. LeBron scored as many points alone as the opposing team scored total! He averaged more than 30 points per game as a senior in 2002–2003. For the third time since he joined the school, SVSM won the state title.

In 2003, he was named Gatorade Player of the Year for the second time. The award is given to the best high school athlete in a sport in the United States. LeBron was the first person to ever win the award twice.

LeBron takes the ball down the court during a 2003 SVSM game.

LeBron poses for a photo after winning the 2003 Gatorade Player of the Year award.

2003 NATIONAL BOYS BASKETBALL PLAYER
LEBRON JAMES

LeBron holds up his Cleveland jersey
after joining the team in 2003.

Scouts thought LeBron was *by far* the best basketball **recruit** in the country. Some were calling him the best young player since the great Michael Jordan. Most players go to college for at least a year before playing in the NBA. But LeBron chose to skip college. The Cavaliers chose him with the first pick in the 2003 NBA **Draft**. "I'm staying in Cleveland, and I'm real excited," LeBron said.

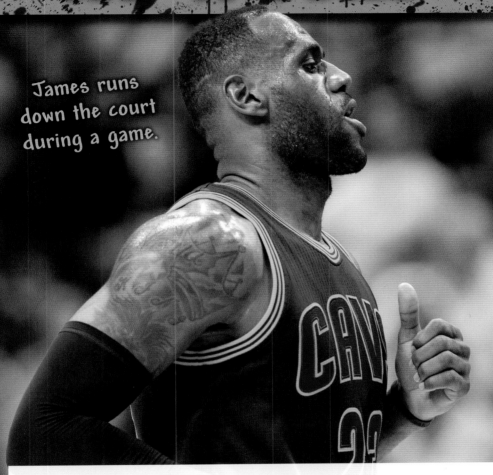

James runs down the court during a game.

James can run faster than most players his size. He jumps higher and stays in the air longer. He can spin and turn more quickly. Natural talent is a big part of his success. But James also works *really* hard to keep his body in top shape.

During the NBA season, James exercises every day. Games and practices keep him busy from fall until spring. He works out a lot during the offseason too: five to seven days a week. If you stop by his house in the morning, don't worry about waking James up. He often rises at 5 a.m. to begin his workouts.

James warms up before a game against Golden State.

A normal day begins with icing and stretching his muscles to keep them loose and prevent injury. He also does **yoga** to strengthen and stretch his muscles. After that, James may head to the gym to lift weights. On other days, he goes to the basketball court. He shoots, dribbles, and practices all the skills he needs during games.

James ices his knees and feet while preparing for a game.

James often wears high-tech gear when he works out. The devices check his heart rate. They keep track of how far he runs and how many **calories** he burns.

James drinks a sports drink
during warm-ups before a game.

Some athletes eat huge amounts of food to keep from getting too skinny. James doesn't eat much more than most people. He starts each morning with two big glasses of water. He likes chicken breasts—without the skin. Pasta, fruit, vegetables, and other healthful foods are also on his menu. He treats himself with pie, pizza, and french fries but never before a game.

With 82 games in the NBA season, James gets sore and tired. He drinks a special mixture after games to help him recover water he lost sweating on the court. The mixture contains water and **carbohydrates** (carbs) his body needs to recover. Then he sinks to the waist in an icy bath. The ice helps his muscles feel less sore the next day.

If the game was in another city, James and his teammates usually hop on an airplane after leaving the arena. Even in the air, James continues working on his body to get ready for the next day. He receives a massage and wears special clothing to get his blood flowing. Electronic devices make his muscles twitch to keep them loose. A careful postgame diet with lots of carbs flushes **toxins** from his body. His career depends on his body, and James works hard to keep it running.

James appeared
on *Good Morning
America* in 2016.

James is surrounded by cameras as he runs onto the court for a 2014 scrimmage in Cleveland.

LeBron James is one of the rare athletes who fans know instantly by just his first name. He's the top player in the NBA and a worldwide sports celebrity. In recent years, his star power has surged way beyond the basketball court.

James poses for a photo during his 2016 appearance on *Good Morning America*.

King James, as he's known to fans, can often be seen on TV. And not just during Cavs games. James has appeared on TV shows from *Good Morning America* to *The Tonight Show Starring Jimmy Fallon*. He hosted *Saturday Night Live*. He even voiced himself on an episode of *The Simpsons*.

He's been popping up on the big screen lately too. Older audiences thought he was really funny when he played himself in the 2015 movie *Trainwreck*. Some **critics** even said he stole the show. Fans of all ages will look for him in the upcoming movie *Space Jam 2*.

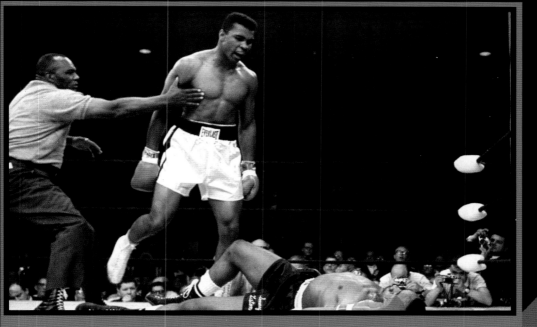

Boxer Muhammad Ali has appeared on the cover of *Sports Illustrated* 40 times.

21

Companies are eager to work with James. He has helped sell products for Coca-Cola, Dunkin Donuts, and many others. In 2015, he agreed to a lifetime deal to represent Nike. It was the first time the company had agreed to such a long deal with an athlete.

With money from the NBA, Nike, and others, James is rich. In 2015–2016, he earned $77.2 million. That made him the third-highest paid athlete in the world.

James spent some of that money on a six-bedroom home in Akron. The house has a huge game room and plenty of space for his family. In 2013, James and Savannah Brinson got married. The couple began dating when they were both in high school. They have three children: LeBron Jr., Bryce, and Zhuri. LeBron Jr. is already a force on the basketball court at the age of 12.

James laces up Nike shoes before a game.

James poses with kids at a LeBron James Family Foundation event.

There are rumors that some college teams have already offered him a place on their teams.

James is closely connected to his community. He uses his star power and money to make Ohio a better place. The LeBron James Family Foundation works to strengthen communities and promote education. In 2015, the foundation planned to give college **scholarships** to 1,100 students. The cost of that many scholarships is more than $40 million.

James helps the Cavs beat the Detroit Pistons in 2005.

The 2002–2003 Cleveland Cavaliers were tied for the worst record in the NBA at 17–65. Then they drafted James. The 2003–2004 Cleveland Cavaliers were better. They ended the season 35–47. James was voted **Rookie** of the Year.

The Cavs got better each year with James. In 2006–2007, he helped the team reach the NBA Finals. But the San Antonio Spurs beat them in four games.

After the 2009–2010 season, James announced he was leaving Cleveland. The news crushed Cavs fans. He joined a group of stars on the Miami Heat. James, Dwyane Wade, and Chris Bosh were a mighty force on the court. The Heat won the NBA championship in 2011–2012 and 2012–2013. With two titles, James had reached the peak as an NBA player.

Could James play in the National Football League (NFL)? Many people would like to find out. Since he played as a child, rumors of giving the sport another try have always followed him. In 2015, James put the rumors to rest and said he wouldn't play in the NFL. "Love it still though," he wrote on Twitter.

James answers questions during a 2014 event held in Akron to welcome him back to Cleveland.

King James returned to Cleveland for 2014–2015. When he and the Cavs won the title in 2016, his place as a basketball legend was secure. He has been voted to 12 NBA All-Star Games, and he has been named league Most Valuable Player (MVP) four times. If he retired tomorrow, he would be remembered as an all-time great. But James is barely more than 30 years old. He still has years to reign as the king of the NBA.

James poses with his 2012 MVP trophy.

All-Star Stats

James was 31 years of age at the beginni
season. He already ranks high on the NE
Yet many NBA stars play into their late
James compares to some of basketball's
the time he retires, he'll likely be a lot h

Most Points Scored by a Player in a C

Player	Point
Kareem Abdul-Jabbar	38,38
Karl Malone	36,92
Kobe Bryant	33,64
Michael Jordan	32,29
Wilt Chamberlain	31,41
Dirk Nowitzki	29,49
Shaquille O'Neal	28,59
Moses Malone	27,40
Elvin Hayes	27,31
Hakeem Olajuwon	26,94
LeBron James	26,83
Oscar Robertson	26,71
Dominique Wilkins	26,66
Tim Duncan	26,49
John Havlicek	26,39

*Through the 2015–2016 NBA season

Source Notes

7   Dave McMenamin, "LeBron Finally Brings a
    Title Home to Cleveland," *ESPN*, June 11, 2016,
    http://www.espn.com/nba/playoffs/2016/story/_/
    id/16347923/nba-playoffs-2016-lebron-brings-title
    -home-cleveland.

8   Buzz Bissinger and LeBron James. *LeBron's
    Dream Team: How Four Friends and I Brought a
    Championship Home* (New York: Penguin Books,
    2010), 17.

12 Tom Canavan, "Cavaliers Win LeBron James
    Sweepstakes," *Pittsburgh Post-Gazette*, May 23,
    2003, http://old.post-gazette.com/sports
    /other/20030523cavsjamesso6.asp.

25 Micah Peters, "The 10 Most Interesting Parts of
    LeBron James' Twitter Q&A," *USA Today*, July 28,
    2015, http://ftw.usatoday.com/2015/07/10-most
    -interesting-parts-of-lebron-james-twitter-qa.

Glossary

calories: units of energy

carbohydrates: substances in food that the body needs for energy

critics: people who judge art such as films and books

draft: a yearly event in which teams take turns choosing players

dunk: to throw the ball through the basket with the hands above the rim

free throw: an unopposed shot taken from the free throw line

recruit: a player who is being considered for the next level

rookie: a first-year player

scholarships: money given to students to help them pay for school

scouts: people who judge the skills of basketball players

three-point basket: a shot worth three points that is taken from behind the three-point line

toxins: poisons

yoga: exercise that includes careful breathing and body control

Cleveland Cavaliers
http://www.nba.com/cavaliers

Fishman, Jon M. *Kyrie Irving*. Minneapolis: Lerner Publications, 2017.

Gitlin, Marty. *Playing Pro Basketball*. Minneapolis: Lerner Publications, 2015.

The LeBron James Family Foundation
http://lebronjamesfamilyfoundation.org

The Official Website of LeBron James
http://www.lebronjames.com

Savage, Jeff. *Super Basketball Infographics*. Minneapolis: Lerner Publications, 2015.

Index

Photo Acknowledgments

The images in this book are used with the permission of: © iStockphoto.com/63151 (gold and silver stars); Karen Schiely/TNS/Newscom, p. 2; MARCIO SANCHEZ/POOL/EPA/Newscom, p. 4; JOHN G. MABANGLO/EPA/Newscom, p. 7; AP Photo/Amy Sancetta, p. 8; Seth Poppel Yearbook Library, p. 9; AP Photo/Bruce Schwartzman, p. 10; AP Photo/Greg Ruffing, p. 11; AP Photo/Tony Dejak, pp. 12, 19; © Wesley Hitt/Getty Images, p. 13; © Thearon W. Henderson/Getty Images, p. 14; © MARK RALSTON/AFP/Getty Images, p. 15; AP Photo/Wilfredo Lee, pp. 16, 27; Everett Collection/Newscom, pp. 18, 20; AP Photo/File, p. 21; © Ezra Shaw/Getty Images, p. 22; © Aaron Davidson/Getty Images, p. 23; Icon Sports Media 441/Icon Sports Media/Newscom, p. 24; © Angelo Merendino/Corbis/Getty Images, p. 26.

Front cover: Karen Schiely/TNS/Newscom; © iStockphoto.com/neyro2008.